FAVOURITE LAKELAND WALKS

Hope you enjoy the walks
Best wishes

Michael

MICHAEL SHINE

GW00514715

A selection of favourite walks with shortcuts and sketch maps

M.M. Publishing

Published by

M.M. Publishing

© Michael Shine

First published 2002

ISBN No. 0-9543407-0-1

Published by M.M. Publishing
Longridge, Sawbridgeworth Road, Hatfield Heath, Essex CM22 7DR
Edited by Laurie John
With thanks to Hannah Shine & Adrienne Tinn for their help
Front page photograph by Howard Moore
Back page photograph by Michael Shine
Graphics & printing by M&B Print Solutions, Gt Dunmow, Essex

Preface

I have two qualifications for writing a preface to this new book of walks in the Lake District. First, I have been stuck half way up Swirrel Edge on the flanks of Lakeland's Helvellyn in Wellington boots so I know how valuable an authoritative book of walks would have been. Second, I have the pleasure of being well enough acquainted with Michael Shine to know that before he takes a break anywhere in the world, he studies all the guide books and works of reference so that when he gets to his destination, he doesn't miss a thing.

To the walker, there are three Lake Districts stacked one on top of the other. There is the Lake-land seen from the level of Wordsworth's daffodils. This is the haunt of the day tripper, a visual feast with enchanting small towns dipping their skirts in sparkling waters extending as far as the eye can see, all set against a back-drop of fells glowing green and blue in the sun, whilst beyond tower mysterious peaks. An hour's climb up the fells reveals a matchless view of entire lakes nestling in a congregation of mountains, each different in character. Half a day's walk and climb to the very top of a mountain may produce a surprise. All the lakes have disappeared! Except, perhaps, for a glimpse of blue extending beyond a tall headland far below.

Having scrabbled my way dangerously to the top of Helvellyn all those years ago my main memory of the summit was the sight of a man and wife who were just departing. Hardened hikers both, they were bickering at each other as they walked nonchalantly down the route I had just crawled up as if it was just a flight of stairs. This book is not for them, at least, not primarily. I almost wrote that it is for those of us who wonder whether we ought to be out walking at all, but that would miss the point.

Here is a book of walks written by an observant man who loves beauty. He hates to waste his time, and would not dream of wasting yours. So let him take you for a walk or two. I promise you will not be disappointed.

Laurie John

Yearning for the Lakes

I weary for the fountain foaming,
For shady holm and hill,
My mind is on the mountain roaming
My spirit's voice is still.

I weary for the woodland brook
That wanders through the vale,
I weary for the heights that look
Adown upon the dale.

The crags are lone on Coniston
And Glaramara's dell,
And dreary on the mighty one
The cloud enwreathed Sca-fell.

Oh, what although the crags are stern.
Their mighty peaks that sever,
Fresh flies the breeze on mountain fern
And free on the mountain heather.

I long to tread the mountain head
Above the valley swelling,
I long to feel the breezes sped
From grey and gaunt Helvellyn.

There is a thrill of strange delight
That passes quivering o'er me,
When blue hills rise upon the sight
Like summer clouds before me.

John Ruskin

CONTENTS

INTRODUCTION

These walks encompass a wide range of terrain from valley to woodland, and to lower fellside. Though they are written for people arriving at the start by car, most of the walks are accessible by public transport. It is a good idea to obtain a bus timetable from the bus stations in the towns or, sometimes, from the bus driver.

Some of the walks are split into sections so that you needn't do the full walk. Others are short enough to fill a spare couple of hours. All these walks allow you to enjoy the breathtaking magic of the Lakes.

HOW LONG WILL IT TAKE? SHALL I BE BACK IN TIME TO CATCH THE BUS OR TO DRIVE BACK IN TIME FOR MY MEAL? Those are the first questions the walkers ask, but depending on your age and fitness, the time needed for these walks can vary considerably.

I shall indicate at the start of each walk two or three different estimates. The first will be the time it takes to complete the walk at a steady, but not too hard, pace (or to complete the first section that allows you to cut the walk short). The second will be the time to complete the same distance allowing a slow pace and time to rest and admire the view. The third is the time to finish the complete walk at a slow pace allowing one to two hours of breaks for picnics and so on.

When I lead groups of people on the complete walks at a moderate pace I normally allow two hours for breaks because everyone seems to have different opinions of where they would like to stop and admire the view, and everyone needs to be satisfied! Two hours is generally ample for toilet and refreshment breaks when there is a larger group.

The degree of difficulty of walks is always subjective but I have listened to the opinions of people whom I have guided on these walks, and blended them with my own. For those who are fit all these walks will be fairly easy, even on the occasional strenuous part. For myself (not so fit, middle-aged and with a knee that doesn't always do what I want it to) none of the walks are difficult.

Any view that would make a good photograph I have shown on the walks as (photo).

Nearly all National Trust car parks are pay and display. National Trust members can park free in these car parks, and need only to display their membership card.

DOS AND DON'TS

Easy as some of these walks may be I recommend that you always wear proper footwear. Shoes and boots should fit properly, preferably be waterproof and have cleated or ridged soles. Never wear smooth soled shoes because these do not provide grip even on dry grass. By far the largest proportion of accidents on the fells happen due to inappropriate footwear. It is also better to wear woollen walking socks which greatly reduce the likelihood of blisters.

This is the "Lake" District so it follows that the area receives a lot of rainfall. This can create boggy areas. They are usually noticeable by being brighter green than the area around them or by being mossy. A general rule to use when trying to avoid these is that heather and bracken do not grow in bog.

Wearing layers of clothing is always recommended as the temperature can change quite quickly, but these walks do not go high enough to get the extreme changes you can experience between valleys and felltops.

A small rucksack is all you need to carry your waterproofs and a drink and light bite. Food and drink are not really required on these walks but they are handy if the weather is hot or you decide to take your time and admire the view. Always use a rucksack instead of bags so that you have your hands free and are much better balanced.

The walks in this book are descriptive enough for you not to need a map but it is a good idea to get a one inch to the mile (1: 63360) map. It covers all these walks, which enables you to see how they relate to each other, and also helps you to identify landmarks of interest.

Always keep dogs under control - remember, farmers are legally allowed to shoot dogs found worrying sheep.

Always close gates behind you.

Don't leave your litter behind; take it away with you.

Don't pick plants; leave them for others to enjoy. Don't attempt to break the main stems of bracken with your hands - the broken parts can be razor sharp!

I think the old adage is worth following: 'If you have a chance to use a toilet, do so'. It may be 'inconvenient' not to!

If you are walking on your own, even though these walks are fairly easy and there are usually other people around, it is good practice to let someone know your route. A lot of hotels, guest houses, etc. provide little printed forms for you to fill in for this purpose. Your safety and well-being is paramount.

You are about to set off on some of my favourite walks but they have also been chosen as favourites by people whom have accompanied me over the past 25 years.

...Enjoy them.

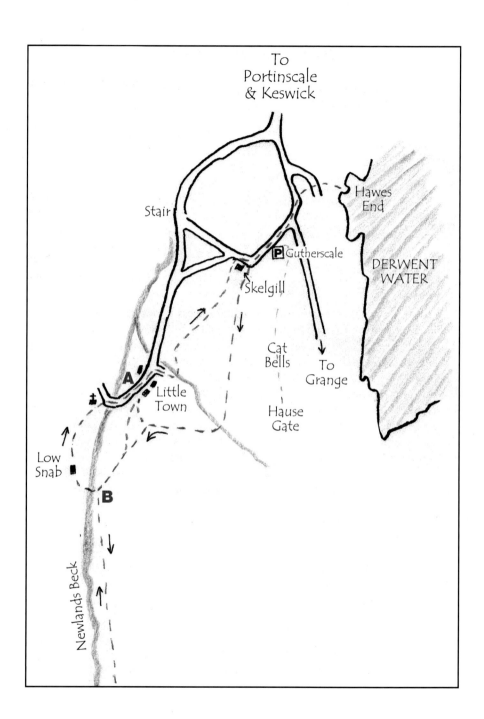

To
Portinscale
& Keswick

Stair

Hawes
End

P Gutherscale

DERWENT
WATER

Skelgill

Cat
Bells

To
Grange

A

Little
Town

Hause
Gate

Low
Snab

B

Newlands Beck

NEWLANDS VALLEY

This is an easy low-level walk of 3 to 7 miles but part of it can be very muddy early in the year or if there has been heavy rain. It is, otherwise, a peaceful walk in very tranquil countryside.
Steady pace: 1½ hours. Slow pace: 2½ hours. With breaks: 5 hours.

There are two ways to start this walk. You can catch the ferry from Keswick to Hawse End Landing (10 minutes) and walk uphill along the path to the road. Then continue up the winding road and across a cattle grid on to the junction where you go down the narrow road to Skelgill Farm. Or you can drive to Gutherscale car park (about 15 spaces) in the narrow road at the northern end of Cat Bells (just off the road between Portinscale and Grange), or park (safely) along the road.

Come out of Gutherscale car park and walk further down the narrow road. A sign shows it as a dead end road to Skelgill Farm. Just before the wooden gate into the farm there is a metal gate saying 'Agricultural Access please keep clear'. There is a wooden post alongside with a sign 'Public Footpath Permitted Cycle Route' and this is the route you should take. There is a steady incline uphill and as you go up you will get a good view down the first part of Newlands valley (photo) and up High Craggs to Hindscarth and Robinson to the right of it, with Knott Rigg further over. Cat Bells is up to your left and as you travel along the foot of it you will probably see people walking along the crest looking like Lowry people - matchstick men and women. If you face the way you came Skiddaw is the highest mountain you can see with the end of Bassenthwaite Lake to its left. This is the only 'Lake' in the Lake District! All the other bodies of water are called 'Mere', 'Water' or 'Tarn'.

This is a peaceful walk along a good path and you will see a cluster of white buildings down to your right that live up to their name of Little Town. You may also be able to hear Newlands Beck running in the bottom of the pretty valley. When you come level with the end of Cat Bells the path slopes gently downwards to the remains of the old mine spills and across a bit of the old cobbled yard of the mine. There are paths that go up to the left towards Hause Gate at the end of Cat Bells where there are some of the old, fenced off, mine workings. If you go up there make sure you keep children away from them.

Carry on across the cobbles until you reach a little beck and then left alongside it for a few yards until you reach where the path crosses it. You have to walk across some stones in the water but it is only a couple of inches deep.

You are now walking along the track with Cat Bells behind you and a good view (photo) along the valley towards Bassenthwaite. A little further on, the track makes a sharp right bend downhill to Little Town. If you decide that this is the furthest point you wish to go on the walk then continue down into Little Town and pick up the return route shown at (A) later on - which will give you a total distance covered of three miles from Gutherscale car park. Otherwise, at the sharp right bend in the track, go off to the left - on the grass - and you will then see a distinct grass track going further into the valley. You can also pick up this part of the walk by going down the original track to Little Town and then turning left along the farm track above the road.

Continue down the grass track. You will see the farm track, and the road, down to your right with the road going over a narrow bridge across Newlands Beck. The two tracks meet and you continue up the valley to your left. The track runs parallel to a wall on your right for just over half a mile. Where the wall turns right is now the time to make your next choice of routes (B). You can follow the track that continues right up to the head of the valley and up to Dale Head, 2473 feet, (not part of the walk). This is a fairly level walk for about 1½ miles to a waterfall that is quite spectacular when there has been a lot of rain. On large scale maps the waterfall is called 'waterfall'! Then retrace your way back to where the wall turned right. Otherwise you just follow the wall to a bridge across Newlands Beck. Just before the bridge, and to your left, there is a low rock in the grass that is quite comfortable for sitting and having some refreshments whilst watching the beck bubbling in front of you.

Cross the bridge and through a gate and then branch slightly left and uphill towards wooden posts which bring you on to the track. You can go straight ahead alongside the wall but if it is wet this can be quite slippery. Turn right onto the track and walk the short distance to Low Snab Farm and through the farmyard gate. Sometimes refreshments are available and eggs are for sale. You may also be greeted by chickens and a dog or two. Carry on through the farm, down the road and out through the gate.

You will cross a small bridge - look out for a tyre track mark in the top of the bridge wall on the right. Ahead is Newlands Church with the tiny schoolhouse attached to it. Go through the gate and turn right on to the road. Walk over the bridge, across Newlands Beck which you saw on the way up the valley, and follow the road uphill to Little Town.

(A) Go the short distance through Little Town and, just as you come out of it, turn right up the track signposted, 'Public Footpath - Skelgill one mile', which can be very muddy in wet weather. Continue through the gateway, over the little bridge and along the track between the hedgerows which in late summer are covered with sloes - useful for making sloe gin!

Follow the path through gates and over stiles and then across a field on a grass track with a row of hawthorn trees on your left. Continue towards the wall with a ladder stile. Go over the wall and on to Skelgill farm. Pass through the farm to the road and turn right uphill, then through the gate back down the road to where you started.

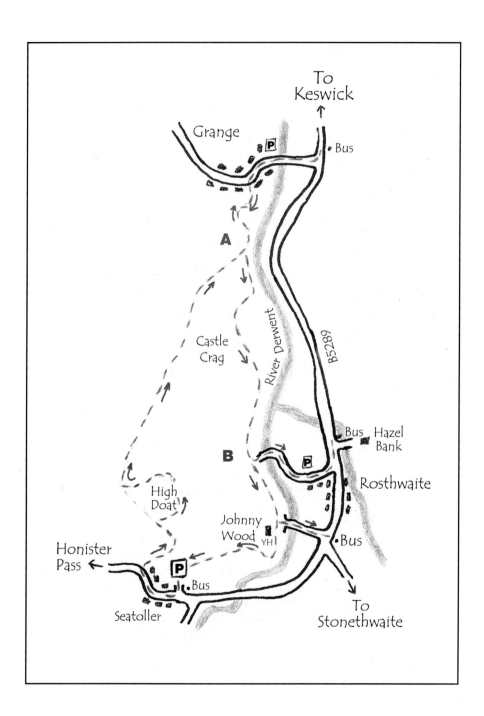

To
Keswick

Grange

Bus

A

Castle
Crag

River Derwent

B5289

Bus Hazel
Bank

B

Rosthwaite

High
Doat

Johnny
Wood YH

Bus

Honister
Pass

Bus

Seatoller

To
Stonethwaite

BORROWDALE - SEATOLLER
HIGH DOAT - CASTLE
CRAG - GRANGE - ROSTHWAITE

A combination of walks from 3 to 6 miles that are mostly easy with a mildly strenuous, but easy, stretch up to High Doat.
Steady pace: 2 hours. Slow pace: 3 hours. With breaks: 6 hours

High Doat, at just over 900 feet, has one of the most picturesque views in the Lake District (see front cover) and it is an ideal walk on a clear day.

The walk starts at Seatoller National Trust car park which can be reached by travelling south on the B5289 from Keswick or through Honister Pass from Buttermere. A bus also runs regularly from Keswick to Seatoller car park. Look out for the large variety of friendly chickens, and the occasional duck or turkey, that come begging for food when you park your car. There are toilets in the car park.

Turn right out of the car park and upwards along the road towards Honister Pass. On your right will be Seatoller Barn, a tourist information centre that also has an interesting display of the history and geology of the valley. Opposite the Barn is The Yew Tree restaurant dating from 1628 - well worth a visit. You can enjoy either a meal or tea and coffee indoors, surrounded by a very interesting display of memorabilia, antiques and photographs, or in their pretty garden.

Continue up the road and after about 150 yards there is a gateway on the right - opposite a car turning area. Go through the gateway and follow the path upwards. After a short distance you will go through another gate (photo). There are good photographic opportunities from here if the lighting is right - especially of the little hamlet of Seatoller. A little further up the path veers sharply to the left and comes to a gate in a wall. Go through the gate but do not follow the path onwards. Instead turn right keeping the wall on your right and shortly go through another gate. You will now be on open fellside of grass and bracken which is the side of High Doat. Follow the faint path curving upward to the left. The path is easy to follow up and down as it gradually wends its way up the hillside. When you go through the next gate the path begins to get a little steeper and when you come to a fork in the path you continue uphill on the left fork. The right fork will take you down to Johnny Wood (a Sight of Special Scientific Interest for the fungi that grow there). The wood has predominantly sessile oak (very short oaks and not the large magnificent trees normally associated with the word oak).

The path here becomes steeper again but you are now very near the top. The top of High Doat is a group of hillocks of grass and bracken and you can wander up on to any of them. This is a perfect place to sit and admire the magnificent views (photo) - and have a drink and a bite. If you enjoy painting landscapes you could spend the whole week up here.

You now have a 360 degree panoramic view. Look north up the valley and you will see part of Derwent Water with Keswick and Skiddaw in the background. Castle Crag, a very popular climb, is in the middle of the valley ahead between what is known as the Jaws of Borrowdale. Shapes of fells are quite deceptive because Castle Crag looks higher than High Doat but is actually 27 feet lower. To the left of Castle Crag and running back towards you can be seen a wall with a track running along the other side of it. This is the path you will eventually be taking. The village down to your right is Rosthwaite and you can see the path (the one you will take in Walk 5) that runs up the hill behind the village and over to the pretty hamlet of Watendlath.

By now you will have covered no more than a mile but it is mainly downhill from here. To continue on the walk you need to follow the grass path to the left, (when facing Castle Crag), through the hillocks of High Doat. This will then start down to the left. At first it looks steep but there is a narrow path for just about 10 yards and then you come to a stile. Go over the stile and follow the wide grass path that winds downhill (it can be muddy at the bottom). You are aiming for the large ladder stile over a wall in the distance which will take you on to the track that you detoured from near the beginning of the walk. Go over the stile and turn right - if you turn left you can be back in Seatoller in 15 minutes.

Follow this track through gates and over small bridges and you will eventually come to Castle Crag. The track starts downwards here but it is worth stopping to admire the view (photo) of Derwent that has opened up before you. There are some nice flat rocks to sit on. The wide track takes you down past Castle Crag to the woods and the river (photo). This is where you have your first choice of different routes (marked 'A' on the sketchmap). In either case it is worth making a short stop by the River Derwent before going on.

CHOICE 1

This will end your walk in just over half a mile. Carry on along the bank with the river on your right for just a short distance and then go left towards a stone wall. At the wall walk along the track with the wall on your right. You will, in a short distance, come to a road crossing your path. Follow this round to the right into the village of Grange. Turn right at the road and a little further on, past a cafe, you will see a sign for the public toilets. A little further on, past the teashop the road bends round to the right and over the double bridge (photo) across the river. The bus stop is across the bridge on the opposite side of the road. It is a good idea to check the time of the bus - Grange to Seatoller - before settling down to enjoy the excellent soup, cakes or ice creams at the teashop.

The bus - usually every half hour or hour depending on season - takes you back to the car park at Seatoller.

CHOICE 2

You can, of course, have a break in Grange and then retrace your steps the short distance back to the river and then join up with the rest of the walk.

To carry on to Rosthwaite and Seatoller go a very short distance back into the woods the way you came where there is a path (now to your left) signposted to Rosthwaite with a yellow waymarker and another sign with a blue waymarker to Seatoller (that is where you just came from). This walk takes the Rosthwaite path. Follow the path through the woods and it goes alongside the river for a short distance. Follow the gravel path curving to the right and away from the river, signposted 'footpath'. Continue on the path as it curves to the right and becomes a stone path towards the woods and a wall. Move on alongside the wall and after a short distance go through the gap in the wall (not the gap at the bottom of the wall).

Continue on the path up through the woods and you will be able to see Castle Crag up to your right. The path then winds downhill again. Just after you start down there is a path to the left - take this one and go downhill through the gap in a wall. Go through the slate spills - but be careful if it is wet. At the fork in the path take the wider right-hand path. The narrow one to the left just goes to the river.

Go through the gate and out of the woods into a field (photo). The woodland ahead of you is Johnny Wood. Across the field and through the next gate you will come to a bridge across the river, (marked 'B' on the sketchmap). If you cross the river the path goes straight into Rosthwaite, past a teashop, and down the road past the National Trust car park and toilets to the B5289. Opposite you is the village shop. The bus stop for Seatoller is across the road and a short way to your left just by the driveway up to Hazel Bank Hotel. This is also where the walk to Watendlath starts.

CHOICE 3

Instead of crossing the bridge to Rosthwaite (at 'B') continue on the path along the right-hand side of the river, over two small footbridges and on until you reach a farm. The road from the farm and over the bridge goes back to the B5289 (where you can catch a bus the last mile back to Seatoller). The path continues up through the drive of the youth hostel and across the front of the building. Follow the yellow waymarker to Seatoller. On the other side of the youth hostel grounds the path comes to a rock face with an uneven track across it. At one section of the narrow rocky path a chain to hold on to has been driven into the rock face (not suitable for small children). This is only a very short section. Then you come down to a path that turns right by the wall. Follow the path by the wall and you are walking around the edge of Johnny Wood. Follow the path, appropriately signposted 'path', through the gate and you can see the car park ahead of you.

RYDAL AND GRASMERE
FROM WHITE MOSS COMMON CAR PARK

A combination of easy walks from 3 to 4 miles (6 miles if you extend it into Grasmere village) that give good views of these two small but beautiful lakes. Steady pace:1½ hours. Slow pace:2-3 hours. With breaks:4-5 hours.

The walk starts at White Moss Common National Trust car park which is on both sides of the main road (A591) between Grasmere and Rydal. Buses also go to White Moss Common from Grasmere and Ambleside. It is easier to park in the larger car park on the side of the road away from the lakes (on the left when coming from Grasmere). Don't walk out of the car park to the road but go towards the front left-hand side of the car park where there is a path to the left going towards the road. After a few yards, before reaching the road, go on to the grass path to the left into the woods. If you reach the small post-box by the road you have gone too far! A few yards further on it becomes a wide stone path going upwards. This is the steepest part of this easy walk.

Immediately you are on a pretty walk upwards for a few hundred yards through trees and bracken, with some blackberries to be picked in season. Keep alert for the sight, or sound, of deer who frequent this path. At the top of the path you meet a road and opposite you is a small pond full of equisetum which at the right time of year has many small dragonflies flitting backwards and forwards. If you stand with your back to the pond you will see a narrow path just to the right of the path you came up - with a seat at the beginning of it. It is a narrow, rocky, path but worth following for a few yards up to the next bench where there is a superb view across Rydal Water (photo). Retrace your steps back to the pond. At the road turn right and continue along it until it becomes a stone path - this used to be the upper road from Grasmere to Rydal in the old days. Carry on along the path and through a gate following the path through some woods. There is a short rocky bit that goes up and then down. A little further ahead the path splits in two. The left fork is boarded off so carry straight on. Almost immediately the route splits again with both paths running in the same direction. Take the lower one alongside the wall then in few yards fork left back to the upper path - this avoids a rocky bit. You could carry on along the wall but it goes downhill before coming steeply back up to the other path.

Go through a gate and carry on. The next gate brings you out onto a grassy hillside overlooking Rydal Water (photo). There is a wooden bench here for you to sit on and admire the view and nearby is what looks like a stone bench. The 'stone bench'

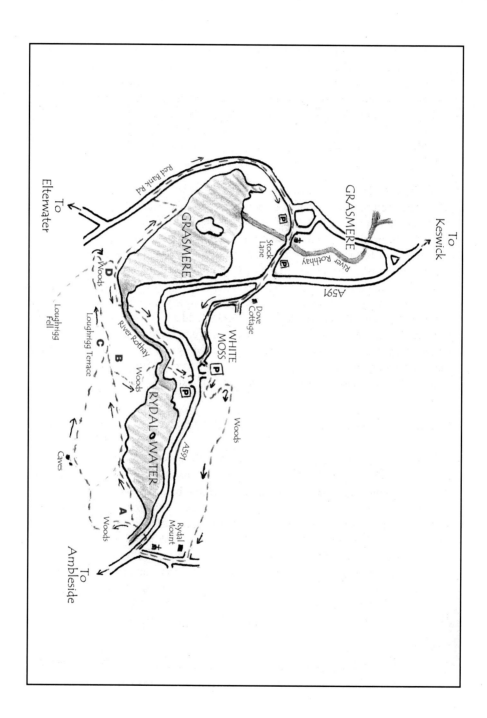

is reputed to be a 'coffin stone'. This goes back to the days when there was no church at Rydal. When someone died they had to carry the coffin from Rydal to Grasmere and the pallbearers used to rest the coffin on this stone. The fell opposite is Loughrigg and you should be able to see the larger of the Rydal Caves in the hillside. Continue along the path and you will soon be walking alongside the upper wall of the garden of Rydal Mount, where William Wordsworth lived for 31 years, and at the end turn right down the road. Rydal Mount is well worth a visit if you have time.

A little further down the road and on the left is a short road to a tea-shop and toilets. Afterwards return to the road and continue on downhill. Just before the main road is Rydal church with Dora's Field behind it. Visitors are welcome. Although Wordsworth originally intended to build a house on this field he never did so and gave the field to his favourite daughter Dora and now it is full of daffodils. The poem 'Daffodils' is sometimes, mistakenly, thought to have been inspired by those in this field but the poem describes a scene near Gowbarrow at Ullswater. The poem was written many years before he moved to Rydal. If you do visit Dora's Field you can go out through the gate at the bottom of the field and it brings you on to the road just by the Badger Bar. Otherwise, at the main road turn right. A short way along, by the Badger Bar (bar meals), cross the road and go through the gap in the wall. Carry on along the path and across the bridge over the River Rothay and then through the gate. Now you have choices - (A on sketchmap).

CHOICE 1 (Otherwise go straight to CHOICE 2)

Go right towards the shore of Rydal Water and through a kissing-gate near the end of the wall. Then through the edge of the woods and out again along the shore with the lake on your right. Here there are tiny, pebble beaches (photo) where children play in the water if it is warm enough (and sometimes when it isn't warm enough). Just a short distance further on, the path bears off to the left, away from the lake, alongside a wall. Continue along the path as it goes uphill and, when you reach the small woods on your right, you will find a narrow gate in the wall (B on sketchmap) which takes you in to the woods. If you take this path through the woods you will, in a short distance, come to another bridge over the river. Cross the bridge and follow the path to the right which brings you into the park area of White Moss Common. The first path to the left leads off to the car parks and the next one to the toilets.

Taking CHOICE 1 is the shortest route. If you decide, when you reach the narrow gate in the wall that you want to carry on further, - instead of going through the narrow gate into the woods carry on up the path the short distance to the brow of the hill and you have joined Choice 3 (C on sketchmap).

CHOICE 2

Instead of going right towards the lake carry straight on to the gate in the wall up ahead and along the path up through the woods. This takes you up a short run of steep steps to another gate. Through the gate turn right along the road and in a short distance you will be on a bridle path. Go through another gate and the view of Rydal Water opens up in front of you (photo). The right-hand path goes down to the shore to meet Choice 1 and the left path carries on up towards Rydal Caves. The path to the caves continues steadily upwards. Woodlands on the left are frequented by deer. Here you come to the first cave, on your left. This cave is not readily accessible so continue on upwards to the much larger cave. At the entrance to this there are two ways in. The, obvious, stepping stones across the water and, the not so obvious, a little rocky scramble along the right-hand side of the entrance. The stepping stones are the best way, unless you have an aversion to crossing water, and you will get an opportunity to see the thousands of tiny fish swimming around the stones. If the natural lighting is right, you can take a good photo looking outwards from the cave using the jagged edge of the roof of the entrance as a frame for your picture.

When you have left the cave follow the path to the left and over a rocky area with a magnificent panoramic view (photo). There are a few different ways down this short rocky area with a bench at the bottom so that you can sit and admire the view. Here you will once again see the route of Choice 1 continue along the path, part of the Loughrigg Terrace, and you will come to a fork in the path. Take the rockier, wider, right-hand path downhill. Ahead you will see that the path meets a wall in the distance. When you come to another fork the path to the right goes across to meet the path in Choice 1 and the gate in the wall to the woods. The left-hand path goes upwards to the brow of the hill and Choice 3.

CHOICE 3

When you have reached the brow (C) of the hill you will see a bench from which you get a lovely view of Rydal Water (photo). In the opposite direction the view across Grasmere will have started to open up. The walk continues on the level path, still the Loughrigg Terrace. As you walk you will see more and more of Grasmere below you (photo) and a small beach by the lake shore. You can see where the path up ahead eventually reaches a wall and some woods. Just before the end of the Terrace there is another path, with rock steps, going up to your left. This will take you up on to the top of Loughrigg, 1099 feet, approx. 700 feet above you. Although this is not part of the walk, for those of you who are feeling energetic, this is not a difficult route.

The walk continues on through the gate at the end of the Terrace and then through a gate on the right in to the woods. Follow the wide zigzag path down through the woods and you will reach the lake. Here you can start on Choice 4 (D on sketchmap). Otherwise turn right, go through a gate and you will be at the beach (photo) that could be seen from the Terrace. Cross the beach and then the bridge. Take the right-hand path through the woods. Cross the field and you will meet the route in Choice 1 where it comes over the bridge into the park area of White Moss Common.

CHOICE 4

Instead of turning right to the beach turn left along the shore. After a short distance the path will turn away from the lake and up to a road - through a wall stile. Turn right onto the road, called Red Bank road, and walk the short distance downhill ($^3/_4$ mile) into Grasmere village. There are plenty of shops, art galleries and eating and drinking places here. To return to the car park go past Grasmere church, along Stock Lane and cross the main road and on to Dove Cottage and the Wordsworth Museum. The route continues past Dove Cottage and when you reach a junction carry straight on. If you turn uphill to your left you will eventually come to the pond with equisetum that you saw at the beginning of the walk. The road eventually comes back to the main road (A591) at the car park. There is usually an ice cream van parked here during the busy season.

To Wrynose Pass

Slaters Bridge

Little Langdale Tarn

Bridge/Ford

Stang End

River Brathay

High Park Farm

Colwith Force

To Coniston

A593

Park Farm

Skelwith Force

Skelwith Bridge

ELTERWATER

Woods

Gt. Langdale Beck

P

ELTERWATER

Britannia Inn

P To Red Bank

To Ambleside

24

ELTERWATER - SKELWITH FORCE - SKELWITH BRIDGE - COLWITH FORCE - SLATERS BRIDGE LITTLE LANGDALE TARN

An easy, and pretty, walk from 4 to 5$\frac{1}{2}$ miles that takes in two waterfalls, two lakes, two interesting bridges and many small woodlands and meadows.
Steady pace: 2 hours. Slow pace: 3 hours. With breaks: 5 hours.

This walk starts in Elterwater village, just to the west of Ambleside. If you drive in from the north the main route is past Grasmere on the A591 to Ambleside and then west on the A593, but there is a much quicker way. Take the first road into Grasmere and when you reach the little village square; do not follow the road round to the left. Instead go straight across into Langdale Rd and at the end turn right into Red Bank Rd (shown on Walk 3). This is a very steep, winding and narrow, road uphill on the west side of Grasmere lake and when you reach the top you take the right turn, by High Close, past the youth hostel and down into Elterwater. This is an interesting drive and, just after you pass the youth hostel, the nature of the countryside changes suddenly from the woodland you have just driven through to a magnificent open view of the Langdales (photo) with Elterwater nestling by the lake below.

There is restricted parking in the village. If you cannot find space in the National Trust car park in the village centre, there is a larger free car park on the northern edge of the village. (If you came over Red Bank you would have passed the free car park on the way down.)

The walk starts in the small car park (public toilets alongside - opposite the Britannia Inn) through the gate on the right and along the path alongside Gt. Langdale Beck. Follow the path over the little wooden bridge, round the edge of the woods and then into the woods, - in the spring there is a wonderful carpet of bluebells amongst the trees. As you walk through the woods you will get the occasional glimpse, through the trees, of the lake with the Langdale Pikes in the background. At the end of the path you reach a wall with a gate in it which leads to an open meadow. Go through the gate and to your right there is a little pebble beach (except that after heavy rain the beach is covered by the lake). If you enjoy feeding ducks and swans this little beach is usually the place to do it. It is amazing how the ducks seem to appear out of nowhere when you have some bread in your hand, - they nest in the reeds opposite. The word 'Elter' is ancient Norse for swan and they are often seen on the lake.

After you have admired the view of the lake with the spectacular panorama of the Langdale Pikes in the background (photo) continue the walk across the meadow following the meandering river Brathay to a gate into the woods. Go through the gate and after about 50 yards the path goes left and up to the road. Do not go that way but take the lower path close to the river and follow it with a wall between you and the road. A little further on the path splits but both paths give you access to Skelwith Force. The right fork goes straight down to it but if you carry on along-side the wall this brings you to steps down to it, which may be easier. Kirkstone Quarries Ltd have erected warning signs, - read them before going to see the waterfalls. Although the Force is not very high it is said to carry more water than any other waterfall in the Lake District, - probably because Elterwater is not only fed by Gt. Langdale Beck but also by Little Langdale Tarn. When you have finished scrambling over the rocks and looking at the falls (photo), either go back to the path the way you came or take the lower path down by the river which also joins the original path by another warning sign.

A little further on the path goes through the yard of the quarry. This is the workshop area of Kirkstone Quarries. They do not do any quarrying here, but you may see them working the slate. Just past the workshops and to the right is their shop (Kirkstone Gallery) and tea shop. A pleasant place to look around. Take your muddy boots off, put them on the rack provided, and enjoy home-made soup and cakes. This is the last place for toilets until you return to Elterwater. If you have your own food with you Kirkstone Gallery have a picnic area you can use down by the river. Go out of the car park and it is on your right.

The walk carries on through the picnic area and turns right across Skelwith Bridge. Keep to the right-hand side of the bridge and follow the road round to the right. Go past the public footpath signed 'Skelwith Force only' and about 150 yards from the bridge take the public footpath to Colwith Bridge. Go through the gate to Bridge How Coppice and follow the yellow waymarker into the woods and, steeply, upwards.

A short distance on you come into the open and carry along the distinct track with views down to your right towards the River Brathay where you walked earlier. Go through the gate to Park Farm. The farmhouse is on your right and, as you walk through the yard, there is an entrance to a barn on your left. In the stone wall to the right of the entrance is a large flat stone with the alphabet carved in it. The origin of this is not known. Opposite the entrance to the barn you will see a yellow waymarker pointing to the continuation of the walk.

Carry on over stiles and through gates. You will come to a house where the path goes through a metal kissing gate, to the left of a wooden shed, and on through another kissing gate. At the time of writing the garden of this house had an interesting, small, terraced garden down to the beck. Continue on to more stiles and gates until you come to a small woodland with a steep path downwards. Take care going down and don't trip on the tree roots. Go across the field at the bottom to the wall with slate steps in it.

Once over the wall you are on the road from Coniston to Elterwater. Turn right and after about 50 yards go left over a stile and follow the sign to 'Colwith Force'. There is a little rocky scramble to the right. Go up it and then the path runs above the river. The path splits a few times but if you keep alongside the river you will eventually hear the rushing of the waterfall. Follow the path to it and there are some rocks you can sit on whilst watching the water drop nearly 50 feet. Colwith Force has two falls as the River Brathay tumbles over them on its run from Little Langdale Tarn to Elterwater.

At this stage, if you do not wish to do the rest of the walk, you can retrace your route the short distance back to the road between Coniston and Elterwater and follow it to the left for just over a mile to Elterwater.

To continue on the walk you can either go on ahead up a little rocky scramble or around the small hill. The path climbs steadily upwards through the woods and away from the river. You emerge from the woods through a gate and turn right alongside the wall. Go through the next gate towards High Park Farm. Usually there are plenty of chickens running free who are quite happy for you to feed them with any scraps of food you might have with you. Having fed the chickens carry on through the farmyard behind the cottages. Then through the gate in the farmyard and out of the gate on to the road.

Turn right down the road and continue along it, ignoring any 'public footpath' signs, and you will come to Stang End Farm. Follow the road as it curves round Stang End. Do not take the road up to Hodge Close but follow round to the left, ignoring the 'public footpath' through the gate. You will now be going down the road with a gate across it and a cattle grid. The road goes over a small bridge and curves round to the right through a small wood. Carry on until you come to a bridge and ford across the river. Do not cross the river but keep going along the track by the left bank.

There are spoils from the old quarry to your left which look as though they have only just been tipped there but in fact they have been there for years. As you go through the next gate you can see Slaters Bridge across the river ahead and to your right. A little further on there is a stile in the wall which leads you across the field to the bridge. It is a small, pretty, bridge of unusual construction in a picturesque setting (photo) and is very popular with artists.

Go across the bridge and follow the path uphill. The view to your left is of Little Langdale Tarn with a panoramic backdrop of fells (photo). Continue through the gates until you reach the farm track and then left to the road. At the road turn left and after a few yards turn right. (If you had not turned right the road would eventually take you to Wrynose and Hardknott Passes and on to the coast. If you intend to drive through these impressive passes make sure that your engine and brakes are in good condition!) Carry on along this road past a farm and the road becomes a track. Over the last ten years I have walked this track there have always been two horses in the field on the left who love to be spoken to and petted. The track becomes a rough stony bridleway which goes all the way downhill to Elterwater. Keep walking straight ahead until you come to a junction. Then turn left along the road, across the bridge over Great Langdale Beck and you are back at the car park and the Britannia Inn.

ROSTHWAITE - WATENDLATH
SURPRISE VIEW - ASHNESS BRIDGE

A medium walk of about 4 to 4^1/$_2$ miles with a fairly easy but steep start as you climb steadily upwards for the first ^{3}/$_4$ mile. This is a popular walk which gives you a variety of scenery with very pretty views.
Steady pace - complete: 2^1/$_2$ hours. Slow pace - complete: 4 hours.
Neither these times include the public transport back.

This is one of the walks which is accessible either by car or public transport. If using public transport you can catch the bus from Keswick to Rosthwaite. If travelling by car you should take the B5289 to Rosthwaite and turn opposite the post office to the National Trust car park. Walk back to the road and turn left. Then cross the road to the small road by the bus stop, signposted Hazel Bank Hotel (mentioned in the 'Rogue Herries' books by Hugh Walpole).

Take the road towards the hotel, across the bridge over Stonethwaite Beck, and just before the entrance to the hotel take the bridlepath signposted to Watendlath and up the track along the left-hand side of the grounds of the hotel. Just as you are passing the hotel, if the water in the streams is high, you can take the upper-level walk along the low wall on your right and it brings you to the gate. Go through the gate and follow the track upwards, through another gate in a wall and continue upwards. Continue through the next gate and look back the way you came to admire the view (photo). There is a good view of the hamlet of Rosthwaite and directly ahead of you is 917 foot High Doat that you climb in walk 2 in this book. The woodland on the side of High Doat is Johnny Wood which comes right down to the bottom of the valley. The valley which can be seen to the left going from the lower end of Johnny Wood goes on to Seathwaite (reputed to have the highest rainfall of any dwellings in England) and then up to the highest mountain in England - Scafell Pike 3210 feet.

You are now just over halfway up and you are walking on what used to be the packhorse route from Rosthwaite to Watendlath. The next part starts off a little bit rough and then comes to a short rocky scramble upwards. This gradually eases off and eventually becomes a smoother track. Do not go on the grass path but keep to the track. Going on the grass just adds to the erosion of the fellside.

Pass through the gate in the wall and go straight on. Do not take the gate in the wall to your right, which goes over to Dock Tarn. The track levels out and then starts

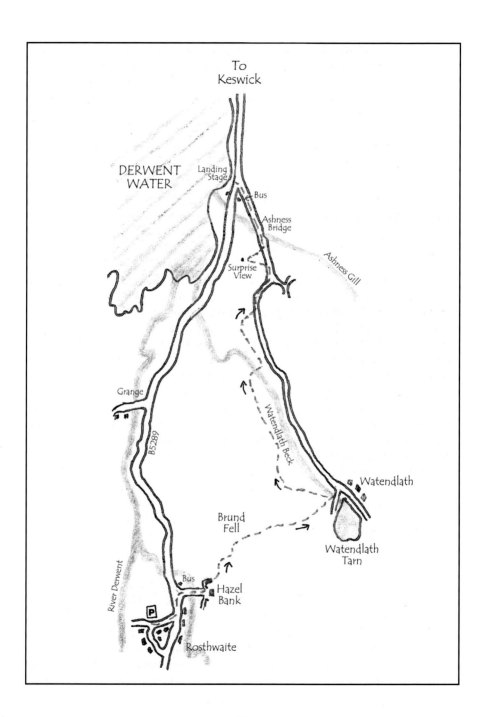

To
Keswick

DERWENT
WATER

Landing
Stage

Bus

Ashness
Bridge

Ashness Gill

Surprise
View

Watendlath Beck

Grange

B5289

Watendlath

Brund
Fell

Watendlath
Tarn

River Derwent

Bus

Hazel
Bank

P

Rosthwaite

downhill to Watendlath. You come to the treeline and then a wall where the path becomes rocky but is easy to navigate. The tarn and hamlet of Watendlath appear down below in front of you (photo). There are toilets there and you can get refreshments. If you have a bite to eat at the cafe be prepared to share it with the finches and chickens.

You now have the choice of returning the way you came or carrying on down the valley to Surprise View and Ashness Bridge.

To carry on to Ashness go back across the pretty bridge (photo) over Watendlath Beck and through the gate to your right. The path runs alongside the beck and there is just a little bit of rock to go over before it turns left away from the beck. A short way further on the path turns right and then runs parallel to the beck.

This pleasant walk alongside the water eventually brings you to some woods and a wall. The path splits left and right and there is a triangular waymarker actually set in the ground. To the left the path goes to Lodore (immortalised in Robert Southey's poem 'The Cataract of Lodore') but you take the path to the right, over the bridge, and through the gate in the wall. You are now following the path on a pretty woodland walk that will bring you to the road between Ashness and Watendlath. Turn left on to the road and follow it for a short distance downhill until you reach a car park in the woods on your right. Turn left into the woods and up a short rocky piece and you are at Surprise View (photo). You will see all of Derwent Water opening out in front of you with Keswick nestling at the base of Skiddaw at the head of the lake. Opposite you, across the lake, is Cat Bells (Walk 6) and Maiden Moor. If you then move down to the lower part on your right, you will be able to look to your left and see further down the Borrowdale valley.

Go back to the road and carry on downhill where you will shortly come to Ashness Bridge (photo). Ashness is one of the most photographed bridges in the country and has appeared on chocolate boxes and biscuit tins for decades. You may find it difficult to get a good photo with all the other visitors trying to do the same.

Continue on the road, steeply, downhill all the way to the main road. The bus stop for going back to Rosthwaite is on the corner of the road. The bus stop for Keswick is just across the road or you can go by launch. To catch the launch you go through a narrow gap in the wall opposite which will take you down some steps to the lake shore and the landing stage. You can either take the launch directly back to Keswick or catch the one which goes round the other way and, eventually, returns to Keswick. The timetables for buses and launches are on the post at the corner of the road.

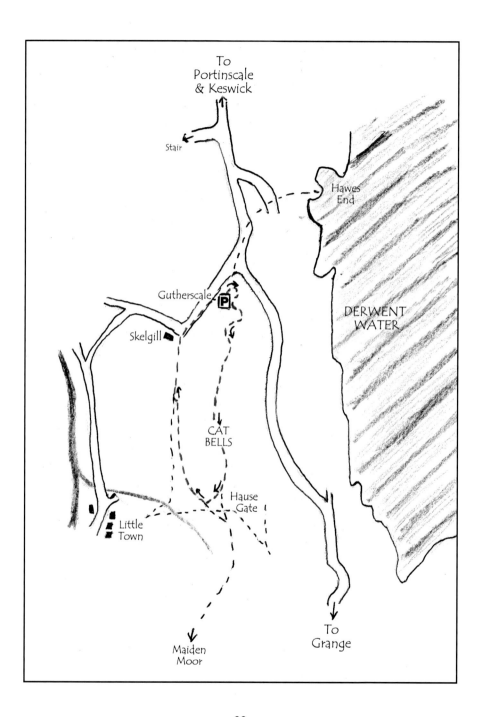

To
Portinscale
& Keswick

Stair

Hawes
End

Gutherscale

Skelgill

DERWENT
WATER

CAT
BELLS

Hause
Gate

Little
Town

To
Grange

Maiden
Moor

CAT BELLS AND NEWLANDS

This is one of those walks where it is essential that you wear good walking shoes and take something to drink and eat as you are bound to want to sit and absorb the wonderful views.

A fairly short walk of just over 3 miles, it gives stunning panoramas of Derwent Water, Borrowdale and Newlands - but do not expect to walk it quickly. It is fairly strenuous with some rocky scrambles but when taken steadily, and carefully, it is not too difficult. (A very reputable magazine, that should have known better, once described this walk as being "for wimps").

With the combination of taking it easy and admiring the view I normally take a good three hours for the round trip.

This is an unmissable walk for a clear day and be sure not to forget your camera - I will not indicate photo opportunities on this walk as the whole walk is one long temptation!

The walk starts from Gutherscale Car Park (as shown on the map, and described, for Walk 1 - Newlands). This time, instead of carrying on along the narrow road, walk back to where this little car park starts and you will see a narrow path which comes downwards into the car park. It is signposted "Cat Bells" and zigzags steeply upwards. At this stage most books of walks just say 'follow the path' because it is so obvious all the way to the other end of Cat Bells but I shall describe some of the ups and downs.

As you ascend you will have wonderful views of Derwent Water opening up in front of you. Keswick is at the head of the lake with Skiddaw behind and you should be able to see the regular ferry service going both ways around the lake. The ferry service can be used not only for this walk and Walk 1 but also for Walk 5.

This is the steepest part of the walk and most people take frequent breaks to 'admire the view'! There is no possibility of getting lost on this path, but please do not be tempted to take shortcuts across the corners as this causes irreparable damage by erosion.

You will shortly come to quite a high rocky scramble which is not too difficult if you take it slowly. There are many ways up so just pick your own. You may feel more comfortable in a few places to use your hands to assist yourself.

Continue up the wide path and as you come over the brow of the hill you will see that there is another hill ahead. The views of Newlands Valley will now be opening up on your right and, to your left, you will be able to see most of Derwent Water. There is a short rocky scramble up this hill and when you reach the top you will see where the path dips down and then steeply upward to the summit of Cat Bells.

If the weather is good you will almost certainly see families, many of them accompanied by their dogs, having picnics on the grass slopes.

The walk up to the summit is also fairly strenuous with some more rocky scrambles. The last time I walked up here I was passed by two six year old girls who appeared to find it quite easy - their parents were struggling up behind us!

At the summit (1482 feet) it is wide and fairly flat and there are now superb views all around. Across Derwent Water, and in the distance, is the Helvellyn range. To the south of Derwent Water you will be able to see Castle Crag sitting in the centre of the Jaws of Borrowdale - part of Walk 2. To the west you are looking down into Newlands Valley and then to the left of Skiddaw is Bassenthwaite Lake.

You can see the path continuing on downwards and then steeply up to Maiden Moor but the walk does not go up there. The dip in the hill between Cat Bells and Maiden Moor is known as Hause Gate. Follow the path down from the summit and as it levels out there is a small grassy path diagonally to the right. After a short distance this path will meet a wider grassy path that has come down from Hause Gate. Follow that path to the right which will take you around the end of Cat Bells and down into Newlands Valley. As you continue to the right Newlands opens up before you and you can see Little Town nestling in the valley below. Those of you who were brought up on Beatrix Potter should keep an eye out for Mrs Tiggy Winkle who might pop out of her front door in the fellside as you walk by!

Continue following the path and you will come to a rocky area and a cairn of rocks. Carry on down over this area of small rocks and you will see ahead of you the path for which you are making. You are now walking on one of the old packhorse trails down from Yewthwaite mines. Follow this path (just one short rocky bit to get down) as it angles downwards all the way along the side of Cat Bells until it meets the large track that takes you back to the car park. This is the track at the start of Walk 1.

GLEN MARY WATERFALL - TOM GILL
TARN HOWS - TOM HEIGHTS

Tarn Hows is reputed to be the prettiest tarn in the Lake District and is one of the best known beauty spots in the country. Although the tarn is partly man made this does not detract from its beauty. Originally there were a few small tarns but the outlet was dammed raising the level of the water and joining the tarns together. Then trees were planted on the islands and around the tarn, creating an unrivalled beauty spot. During good weather (and sometimes bad) you will see many artists painting the lovely scene.

$1^1/_2$ - 2 hours for the described walk and up to 4 hours if you take the easy walks around the tarn and up the hillside across the tarn, plus breaks.

This varied walk of $1^1/_2$ to 4 miles is an easy way to get to see Tarn Hows without the problem of having to take the narrow winding road up to it that is very busy when the weather is good. The first part of the walk is very short and takes no more than 15 - 20 minutes to get from the little car park on the main road up to Tarn Hows.

Park in the National Trust Tom Gill car park which is a small car park in the woods at the bottom of Tom Gill. It is on a bend in the A593 on the Skelwith Bridge to Coniston road about 3 miles south of Skelwith Bridge. About $^1/_2$ mile before the car park there is a small tarn on the right (Yewtree Tarn) and then the car park is on the left, in the trees, just as you approach a right-hand bend. Coming from Coniston it is just over 2 miles. You can be at Tarn Hows quicker by taking this short walk upwards than by driving. If you are unable to park in the car park there are some lay-bys between the car park and Yewtree Tarn.

Start the walk by crossing the small wooden footbridge over Tom Gill just to the left of the car park. Turn right and follow the path alongside the gill. On the short track up to Tarn Hows the idea is to follow the path as near the gill as possible, with the gill on your right, so as not to miss the view of the tumbling waters and the pretty setting for the small waterfall. The National Trust try to protect the paths from too much erosion by diverting you sometimes from the original path. The way is easy and all paths eventually lead back together so you do not miss the waterfall. There is a sign that points the way. As you approach the waterfall the path divides with the main track going straight ahead upwards and a short section that dips down towards the bottom of the falls. This is not difficult but to join the main track by going straight ahead is a bit steep.

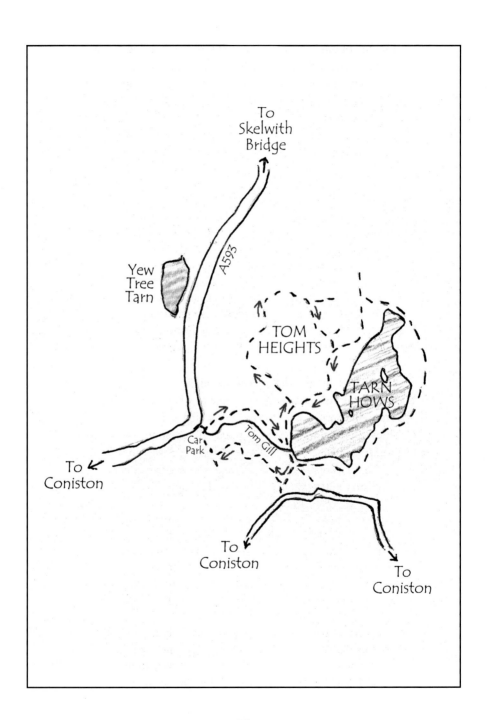

What you see at the bottom is only the lower part of the falls and the rest will come into view further on. The path continues by the falls and then becomes a laid stone track that follows upwards to a kissing-gate. After you go through the gate the path becomes less distinct over a rocky area. Keep on the path by the gill and you will come to a small rocky scramble. You can pick any way over this and will then come to the path as it becomes more distinct again. Once again, where possible, keep near to the gill. As you approach the top of the path from the woodland you will see open sky and come out just by the little dam across the outflow from Tarn Hows.

From here there are many ways to walk and quite a lot of paths. When facing the tarn with the glen at your back you will see paths to your right and running across the grass hill at the end of the tarn. Artists usually do their painting from the upper part of this hill as it is a good vantage point. Paths also run up and across the hill opposite you which gives lovely views of the tarn and towards Windermere. There is a commemoration stone here to Sir James and Lady Scott who donated the Tarn to the National Trust. The path on which you are standing goes around the tarn and is about $1\frac{1}{2}$ miles long. You can take any of these paths depending on how much time you have or how energetic you are feeling but the next part of the walk is along the path you are on.

Tom Heights is a hill up to your left so turn left along the path keeping the tarn on your right. After a short distance you will come to where the land juts out into the tarn and you will see a narrow path to your left which angles uphill. Take this path through the bracken (when in season) and you will come to a short rocky section with some heather growing on it. Although this appears difficult it is not, so continue on. When you reach the top of the rocky section you will have a view across to the Coniston Fells, fronted by Holme Fell opposite.

Follow the path along this ridge. (If you turn round you will see part of Coniston Water in the distance and Tarn Hows down to your left.) Carry on over the little rocky top and take the path down to your left. You are aiming for the hill in front of you with the small stone cairn on the top. When you come to a small, flat, area at the bottom of the path keep to the left as the centre of the flat area can be quite boggy. Remember - heather and bracken don't like boggy areas.

At the cairn Coniston Water can be seen stretching away in the distance. You are now aiming towards the next hill with a cairn on top, and then the next hill with a cairn. If you now look to your right you may be able to see part of lake Windermere and to the north and west the Helvellyn Range and the Langdale Pikes.

From here you will descend, forward, on the grassy path ahead. Where the path levels out there is a good view with the mountains in the background (photo). A little further on the path splits going either straight ahead downwards, or to the right round a rocky outcrop. You can take either path as they meet up again. Further on the path curves to the right and then reaches a fork. The left fork goes towards the path at the end of the tarn - which you can see ahead of you. You will take the right fork.

When you see trees ahead of you and have a rocky hillside on your right take the left path down through the bracken. You are likely to meet other paths in the bracken which all run towards the tarn. Cross a short rocky part and there is a fairly clear path that winds along and downwards which will reach a wide rocky track. Turn right onto this track and in a short distance you will come back to the main path around the tarn. Turn right on the path - signposted Coniston and Car Park. (You can, of course, turn left and follow the path all the way around the tarn.)

When you arrive back at the little dam the way back down to the car park is through the kissing gate just ahead of you. Once through the gate the path splits into three. The path to the left goes along the head of the tarn, the middle one goes up towards the car park and road, and you will take the one to the right.

A little further on take the little path through the bracken off to the right and in a short distance uphill it meets another, wider, grass path on which you turn right. If you had missed the little path through the bracken you would have come to the wider path further on. After a few yards it starts downhill with a wall to your right and then veers left, away from the wall, through some larch trees.

This path zig zags downwards to a gate in the wall. Go through the gate and follow the path keeping the wall on your right. Continue along the path as it winds downwards through the fields and on to another gate in the wall. Go through the gate and turn right down the bridlepath. After a short distance fork right straight into the car park.

Notes

Notes